I0820833

The Story of THE MARY CELESTE

by Noah Leatherland

Roar! Books, an imprint of Bearport Publishing by FlutterBee

Credits
Cover and title page, © Bearport Publishing and © Martin Bergsma/Shutterstock; 4, © Billion Photos/Shutterstock; 4–5, © New Africa/Shutterstock; 6, © Ines/Adobe Stock; 7, © Martin Helgemeir/Shutterstock; 8, © Sarfaraz82/Shutterstock; 8–9, © Alena/Adobe Stock; 9TR, © Public Domain/Wikimedia; 10M, © Hulton Archive/Getty Images; 10BR, © Smith Archive/Alamy Stock Photo; 10–11, © Public Domain/Wikimedia; 12, © Arpad Laszlo/Shutterstock; 12–13, © DenisProduction.com/Shutterstock; 14, © Cmspic/Shutterstock; 14–15, © Bjoern Wylezich/Shutterstock; 16, © Grafvision/Adobe Stock; 17, © Digital Storm/Adobe Stock; 18, © tobibambola/Shutterstock; 19, © BenjiONeill/Shutterstock; 20, © leopictures/Shutterstock; 20–21, © cristi180884/Shutterstock; 22–23, © cgterminal/Shutterstock; 23M, © DEA PICTURE LIBRARY/Getty Images; 23BR, © Luca/Adobe Stock; 24, © Bearport Publishing and © inankilic/Adobe Stock; 25, © Artiste2d3d/Shutterstock; 26, © Public Domain/Wikimedia; 27, © Bogdan Dyiakonovych/Shutterstock; 28, © Fer Gregory/Shutterstock; 28–29, © Rafael Tomazi/Shutterstock; 30, © Voyagerix/Shutterstock; 31, © Martin Bergsma/Shutterstock

Bearport Publishing Company Product Development Team
Kayla Eggert, Theresa Emminizer, Kim Jones, Allison Juda, Naomi Reich, Steve Scheluchin, Tiana Tran

Library of Congress Cataloging-in-Publication Data is available at www.loc.gov or upon request from the publisher.

ISBN: 979-8-89577-843-2 (hardcover)
ISBN: 979-8-89577-851-7 (ebook)

For more information, write to Bearport Publishing, 3500 American Blvd W, Suite 150, Bloomington, MN 55431. Printed in the United States of America.

CONTENTS

HISTORY'S MYSTERIES

Most stories have a beginning and an end. However, some of them leave behind more questions than answers.

These tales have missing information or unlikely endings.

People have tried to solve famous mysteries for many years. Despite their efforts, parts of some of these stories remain unexplained.

Are you ready to explore a mystery?

THE MYSTERY OF MARY CELESTE

The ocean covers 71 percent of Earth's surface. This is why so little of it has been explored.

The ocean is so huge that it's easy to get lost among the waves. In fact, hundreds of ships and their crews have gone missing at sea.

But rarely does a ship appear with nobody on board. However, that's what happened with the *Mary Celeste*.

There are **theories** about what happened to the passengers of the famous ship. But nobody knows for sure.

BEFORE THE MYSTERY

The *Mary Celeste* was a merchant ship that carried goods across the ocean.

NORTH AMERICA

New York City

Genoa

EUROPE

Atlantic Ocean

AFRICA

On November 7th, 1872, the ship set sail from New York City. It was headed toward Genoa, Italy.

There were 10 people on board. This included Captain Benjamin Briggs, his wife, and his daughter.

Benjamin Briggs

The *Mary Celeste* was carrying more than 1,700 barrels of industrial alcohol. However, the ship never made it to Italy.

OUT AT SEA

On December 5th, 1872, the *Mary Celeste* was found drifting at sea. Strangely, there was no one at the wheel steering the ship.

The drifting ship was spotted by Captain David Morehouse and his crew on the *Dei Gratia*.

David Morehouse

This was odd. The *Mary Celeste* had left New York City eight days before the *Dei Gratia*. It should have already arrived in Italy.

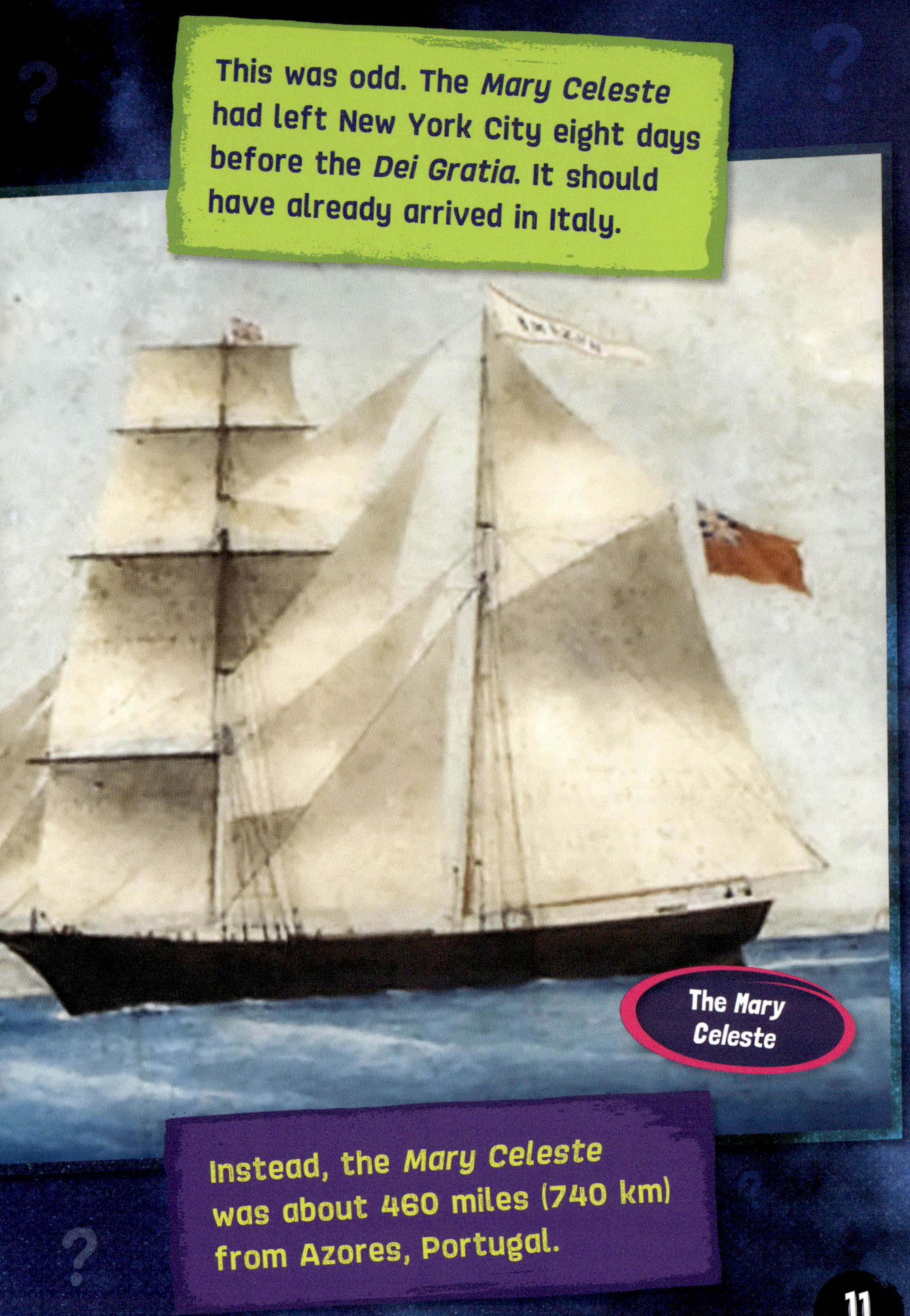

The *Mary Celeste*

Instead, the *Mary Celeste* was about 460 miles (740 km) from Azores, Portugal.

STRANGE FINDINGS

Upon boarding the *Mary Celeste*, Captain Morehouse and his crew were unable to find a single soul. Yet, most of the passengers' things were still there.

There was enough food and water to last at least six months. The cargo was still on the ship, too.

The latest entry on the ship's log was dated November 25th. It said the *Mary Celeste* was coming close to Azores.

The only things missing apart from the passengers were the lifeboat and some navigation gear.

CAPTAIN MOREHOUSE

There were often rewards for bringing lost ships back to a port. So, some members of Captain Morehouse's crew sailed the *Mary Celeste* to Gibraltar.

Gibraltar

But once there, they ran into a problem. People thought sailors on the *Dei Gratia* had something to do with the missing people. They said the men wanted the money.

The officials in charge did an investigation. After three months, they determined that the *Dei Gratia* crew was not involved in the mysterious disappearances.

Despite being cleared, the crew members received only a small amount of the prize money. Some people still thought they were responsible for the missing passengers.

PIRATES

What could have caused everyone aboard the *Mary Celeste* to disappear? Some people think pirates had something to do with it.

Pirates were known for stealing from ships. They were usually looking for something that will make them rich.

But it is very unlikely that pirates targeted the *Mary Celeste*.

Nothing on the ship was stolen. Most of the crew's belongings and the cargo were still on board.

BOOM!

Other people believe there was an explosion on the *Mary Celeste*. The barrels of alcohol might have let out fumes.

If there was a spark, these fumes could have caused an explosion.

Scientists made a model of the barrels and created an explosion with similar fumes. It made a big fireball, but it didn't burn anything down.

If this was what happened, maybe the people on board abandoned the ship.

POISON

One theory says that the crew were poisoned by a type of fungus called Ergot.

Ergot fungus

Ergot can affect the grain used to make bread. Eating food with this fungus can make people hallucinate.

Some people think the bread on the *Mary Celeste* had ergot. The crew may have eaten it and started to see things.

If they saw something scary, they may have run away.

A SEA MONSTER

In the 1800s, people didn't know much about the deep ocean. Even today, most of the ocean remains a mystery.

Some say there could be creatures we don't know about lurking below the waves.

They believed that a giant creature could have attacked the *Mary Celeste*. But scientists say these kinds of monsters don't actually exist.

And if sea monsters were to blame for the missing crew, they probably would have destroyed or sank the ship, too.

THE LEADING THEORY

The leading theory about what happened on the *Mary Celeste* has to do with a sounding rod.

A sounding rod

A sounding rod is a tool that measures how much water is on board a ship.

People think Captain Briggs used his sounding rod incorrectly. He may have thought there was more water on board than there was.

If he thought the ship was sinking, he might have told everyone to abandon the ship.

THE LAST JOURNEY

The crew of the *Mary Celeste* were never found. But the ship did set sail again.

It went through several new owners before the ship took its last journey in 1885.

Gilman Parker was the last captain of the *Mary Celeste*. He crashed the ship just off the coast of Haiti.

Haiti

The *Mary Celeste* was never repaired after the crash. Instead, its broken pieces were left to rot.

FACT OR FICTION?

With so many theories surrounding the *Mary Celeste*, it's hard to tell what is real and what is fake. What are people asking?

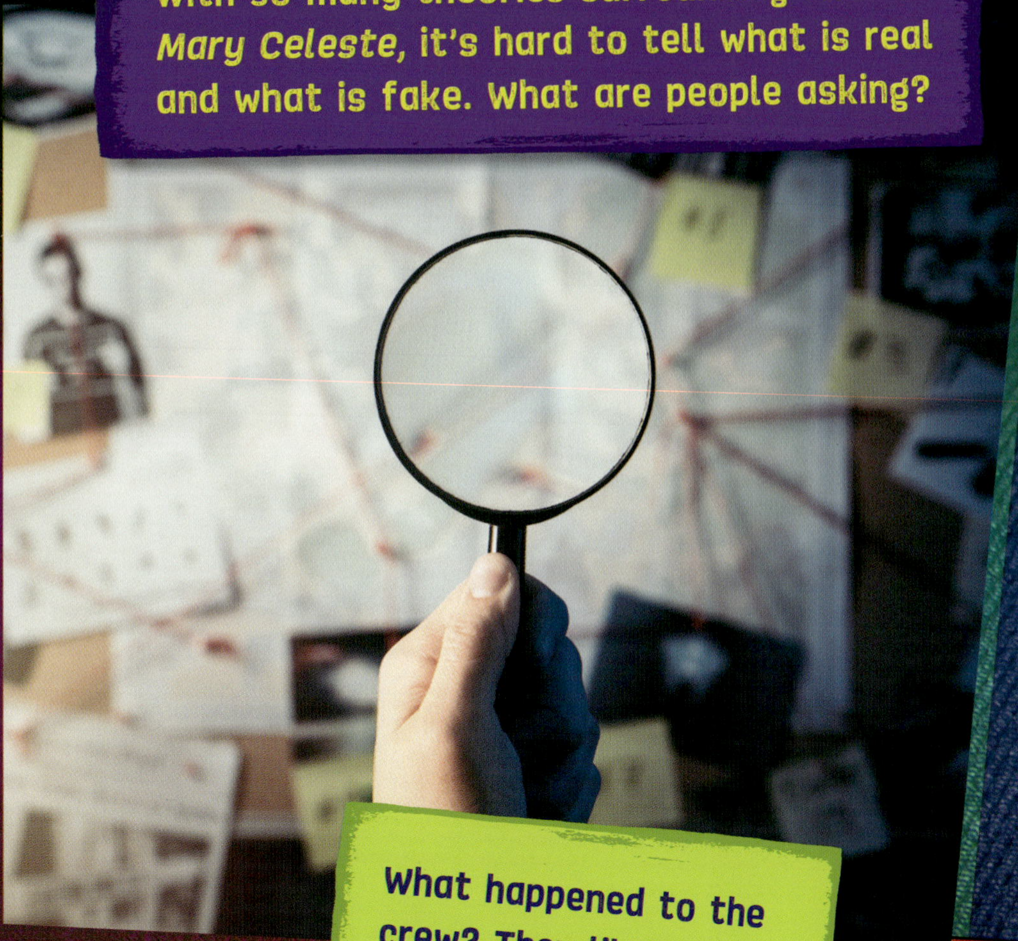

What happened to the crew? They likely left the ship on a lifeboat.

Is the *Mary Celeste* cursed? Some people believe it is because Robert McLellan, the ship's first captain, died on its very first journey.

A lot of claims about the *Mary Celeste* are not true. But the most famous theory is that the crew simply abandoned ship out of fear.

THE TRUTH IS OUT THERE!

There are plenty more clues we might yet uncover to solve the mysteries of the *Mary Celeste*. One day, we might get a step closer to the truth.

It is fun to read about mysteries and wonder about what might have happened. What would you like to explore next?

GLOSSARY

abandoned left alone and uncared for

cargo goods carried on a ship

fungus a plantlike organism, such as a mushroom, that can't make its own food

hallucinate to see, hear, feel, or smell something that does not exist

industrial used in making products

log a written record of events

navigation the act of finding a way around

port a place where ships load and unload cargo

theories ideas used as possible explanations for something

Index

Read More

Amin, Anita Nahta. *The Mary Celeste Ghost Ship (History's Mysteries).* North Mankato, MN: Capstone, 2022.

Williams, Dinah. *Ghost Ship (Unsolved).* New York: Schoolastic, Inc., 2025.

Ziemann, Kimberly. *The Mary Celeste (Unsolved Mysteries).* Mendota Heights, MN: Apex, 2023.

Learn More Online

1. Go to **FactSurfer.com** or scan the QR code below.
2. Enter **"Mary Celeste Story"** into the search box.
3. Click on the cover of this book to see a list of websites.